# THE KISS OF GOD

# James C. Howell

# THE KISS

# OF GOD

## 27 LESSONS ON
# THE HOLY SPIRIT

Abingdon Press
*Nashville*

THE KISS OF GOD
27 LESSONS ON THE HOLY SPIRIT

*Copyright © 2004 by Abingdon Press*

*This book is printed on acid-free paper.*

**Library of Congress Cataloging-in-Publication Data**

Howell, James C., 1955-
    The kiss of God : 27 lessons on the Holy Spirit / James C. Howell.
      p. cm.
    Includes bibliographical references and index.
    ISBN 0-687-06648-4 (pbk. : alk. paper)
    1. Holy Spirit. I. Title.

BT121 .3.H69 2004
231'.3—dc22

ISBN 13: 978-0-687-06648-3

2004003911

07 08 09 10 11 12 13 — 10 9 8 7 6 5 4

MANUFACTURED IN THE UNITED STATES OF AMERICA

*To Jean and Tom Stockton*
*(Mimi and Pop)*
*whose life together in the Spirit*
*has borne much fruit*

# CONTENTS

# A WORD OF INTRODUCTION

When I listen to Christians trying to say what they believe, what they have experienced of God, I notice that some talk quite confidently about the Holy Spirit, as if this Holy Sprit lives right down the hall and is as familiar, as accessible as a lifelong friend. Others do not say so much about the Holy Spirit, for they cannot fathom either the math of a God who is one but also three or the mystery of the ineffable movements of the Holy Spirit.

As a pastor and theologian, I grapple with questions that come to me, such as: Just who is this Holy Spirit? What does the Bible say? What do we believe about the Spirit? And how can I make a connection with the Holy Spirit in my life? What would that look like?

I have written these short lessons, this series of reflections, to help us explore who the Holy Spirit is (and who the Holy Spirit isn't!) and what the shape of life in the Spirit can become. Read, think, pray, wrestle, have a conversation with someone, reflect some more, and perhaps together we will grow in our grasp of the Holy Spirit, or rather, we will grow as we are grasped by the Holy Spirit.

JCH

# WHO IS THE HOLY SPIRIT?

*Come, Holy Spirit, elusive, powerful Wind,*

*Breath of life, closer to me than I am to myself:*

*show Yourself, yet in a way that reminds me*

*that You have always been there, and will always be.*

*So take possession of me; I wait eagerly to learn. Amen.*

In the very beginning, we need to think through the logic of the question: Who is the Holy Spirit? Many might ask: *"What* is the Holy Spirit?"—as if it is some thing, some experience, something you could measure or get your hands on. The Spirit is personal, closer to you than you are to yourself. Grammatically, the Hebrew word *ruach* is feminine, and it means "breath" or "wind." The Spirit is personal, very personal, as personal as your next breath, and yet as elusive as the wind, as invisible as the wind, yet with powerful, noticeable effects.

The very question "Who is the Holy Spirit?" implies another answer: I am not! The Holy Spirit is not me and my spiritual self. I may have had profound, wonderful feelings about God; but the Holy Spirit is far larger than my feelings. I may have had a moving experience authored by the Spirit, but the Holy Spirit is far beyond my experience. The Holy Spirit may (and will!) be the catalyst for startling changes in my life. The Holy Spirit may and will nurture a whole new set of attitudes, will be the spark to ignite an unforeseen passion for God. The Holy Spirit will stir my heart to obey God, to be holy, to be assured of God's unfailing presence. The Holy Spirit will lift me out of my petty life into a heightened consciousness, a delightful intimacy with God that may tempt me to blush, that issues in a sigh.

But the Holy Spirit is not the same as the passion you feel, is not the knee-buckling intimacy. The Holy Spirit is not anything you "have." For the Spirit is too big, too marvelous, too treacherous, to be boxed inside me or you or even the most spiritual person on this planet. The Spirit radically changes my life, precisely because the Spirit is something I can never possess. The Spirit isn't "in" me so much as the Spirit is way ahead of me, behind me, around me, inspiring me and you and the next person, and the space between us. Indeed, the Spirit isn't "in" me because the Spirit is moving all over the universe, creating beauty and light and goodness and love.

This personal, elusive, invisible, powerful Spirit is not something God hurls down from on high. The Spirit isn't a neatly wrapped little package God gives to you, or to me, or to some select group of people. The Spirit ranges widely, showing up everywhere, or the Spirit is nowhere at all—because, again, the Spirit isn't a thing located here and not there. The Spirit isn't something you grab hold of—because the Spirit is God. Talking to the woman at the well in Samaria on the subject of what satisfies our thirst, Jesus said, "God is Spirit" (John 4:24). Who is the Holy Spirit? The Spirit is God, and God is love.

# THE SPIRIT IS LOVE

*Come, Holy Spirit, bearing Your best gift,*

*Yourself; for there is nothing else I need or desire.*

*You loved me though I was unaware, so now I ask*

*You to surprise me once more with that Kiss*

*that tenderly brushes away all loneliness. Amen.*

The Spirit is God, and God is love. When 1 John 4:8 declares that "God is love," we need not infer that everything that pretends to be "love" in our world is somehow divine. "Love" is corrupted, demeaned, cheapened all the time—but our very awareness of this, our intuition that there must be such a thing as genuine, true, eternally unfailing love is a hint about the existence of love, our craving for love, our need to love.

It is no mere coincidence that the first "fruit of the Spirit" is love (Galatians 5:22). But before we get cozy and thank the Spirit for giving us love, or making love happen, we need to refocus our hearts and turn our admiring gaze toward the Holy Spirit, and let ourselves be moved to adoration of this Holy Spirit who quite simply is love, long before love is given or received or even noticed. God the Holy Spirit is love, has always been love, will always be love.

St. Augustine's words move me: " 'The gift of the Holy Spirit' is no more than 'the Holy Spirit.'" Before I plunge into thinking about the benefits of the Holy Spirit, before I weigh the effects of the Holy Spirit in my life or the world, I can be still and revel in the one and only gift of the Holy Spirit that matters, and that is the Holy Spirit itself, herself, himself. Love is like that. When you love someone, you may wrap up a gift and place it under the tree, or you may send flowers, or spend thousands on a diamond ring. But these are mere trinkets, losable, dispensable really. The real gift you give, the only gift you are able to give, is your self.

God the Holy Spirit is like that, loving us, giving us not this or that, but something of immeasurably wonderful value—the Spirit's own self. This kind of love spells the destruction of loneliness. The Holy Spirit's great delight, her consuming passion, his reason to get up in the morning, is to overcome isolation, isolation between me and God, between you and God, between you and me.

Bernard of Clairvaux provocatively suggested that it is appropriate to think of the Holy Spirit as a kiss. He is imagining God the Father loving his son Jesus so tenderly that God would kiss his son, and the Spirit then would be that kiss!—which leads us to consider the Trinity.

# THE SPIRIT IN THE TRINITY

*Come, Holy Spirit, heavenly Dove,*

*inviting us into the love of Jesus and his Father:*

*Take my hand and pull me into the glorious dance,*

*the largesse of fellowship that cannot be contained*

*but must be shared. I want to dance in Your circle. Amen.*

Saint Augustine taught that the Holy Spirit is the bond of love between Father and Son. The whole notion of the Trinity (God as three in one: Father, Son, and Holy Spirit, but still just one God) may befuddle us. But the Trinity is not a mathematical riddle to test our faith. The Trinity is a mystery, but this does not mean the Trinity is irrational. The earliest Christians tried to name their experience of God and to understand the actual story of the Bible as it unfolded.

For instance, when Jesus was baptized in the Jordan, God the Father was overheard speaking from heaven saying "This is my beloved Son." Then at that moment, the Spirit descended on him, like a dove (from Matthew 3:13-17). Jesus, who was quite clearly God in the flesh according to the Gospel of John, spent much time talking about his intimate relationship with his Father in heaven (John 14:10, 16:15, 17:24). Yet he also encouraged the forlorn disciples by promising to send the Spirit once he has gone (John 14:26, 15:26, 16:7). To understand this threefold, divine love, read John 14 through 17 slowly, and with imagination.

Hundreds of theologians have authored thousands of thick books trying to analyze this three-in-oneness in God. But for the believer, what matters is that the Bible suggests that there is an immense, marvelous love within God that spills over into our lives. The Holy Spirit is the outpouring of the love God the Father has for his only Son onto us. The Holy Spirit is the invitation to us to join in the profound love Jesus had (and has) for his Father. There is a beautiful icon by a Russian painter, Andrei Rublev, picturing Father, Son, and Holy Spirit sitting around a four-sided table enjoying each other, with the clear implication that you, the one looking at the painting, you are invited to join their circle. My destiny, your purpose for being, our reason to live: Life is about the privilege, the delight of being invited into the eternal love of God, Father, Son, and Holy Spirit. A kiss is like that. A kiss gently shatters our loneliness, or as Ann Patchett phrased it, a kiss is "like a hand pulling you up out of the water, scooping you up from a place of drowning and into the reckless abundance of air." The Spirit, God's kiss, scoops us up into the air breathed among Father, Son, and Holy Spirit.

Back in the early centuries of Christianity, theologians like John of Damascus and Gregory of Nazianzus, when extolling the wonder of the Trinity, used the image of *peri-choresis*, which can be translated "dance." Dancers move, but together. Dancers allow space, but relate happily to one another. Dancers aren't static, but dynamic, delighting in their mutual, respectful, beautiful, concerted movements. Every time we speak of the Holy Spirit, we must remember that the Spirit is never separated from Jesus or from God the Father. If we believe things about the Holy Spirit that are at odds with what Jesus taught and did, or with what we know about God throughout history, then we are misunderstanding the Spirit. For the Spirit, perhaps uniquely among the divine three, seems determined not to stand out on his own, seems determined never to go her own way, but instead is modest, always diverting attention to Jesus, to Jesus' Father.

# THE BEAUTY OF ANONYMITY

*Come, Holy Spirit. You are beautiful, Lord;*

*You are Beauty. Your shyness moves me to adore You.*

*Weave into my soul that same humble anonymity*

*that looks out from the shadows and into the light,*

*noticing beauty, reveling in humble service. Amen.*

While we are still on somewhat mysterious reflections (and we will move next into more practical matters like how to access the Spirit and the effects of the Spirit), we may ponder the notion of beauty. Think a few minutes about beauty, something you saw that made your jaw drop, some moment that made you sigh, that stammering *ah-h-h* that floats up out of you, tears at the climax of a film: When we are awestruck by beauty, we find ourselves right at a window pane through which, if we turn and look, we may catch a glimpse of God.

The Holy Spirit draws our attention to what is beautiful, partly because the Spirit wants to share her delight in the tender wonders of God's glorious world, but also because God is beautiful. I spoke at a gathering of Pentecostal ministers, and during a joyful, chaotic period of spontaneous prayer, the man next to me swayed as he rhythmically repeated over and over, "You are beautiful, Lord, you are beautiful, Lord. . . . " Jonathan Edwards wrote, "The Holy Spirit is the harmony and excellency and beauty of the Deity. . . . 'Twas his work to communicate beauty and harmony to the world." The thought of God looming over the Milky Way, the memory of the Holy Spirit hovering over creation and your soul, the story of Jesus . . . How does the old German hymn phrase it? "Fairest Lord Jesus . . . thee will I cherish . . . Jesus shines purer than all the angels heaven can boast . . . Beautiful Savior! . . . Praise, adoration, now and forevermore be thine."

But mystics and theologians over the centuries have noticed a peculiar beauty in the Holy Spirit. Notice we never see the Spirit; we have no gender to describe the Spirit; we have no name, few artistic images. Even God the Father has frequently been painted, by Michelangelo, by William Blake. The Holy Spirit is somehow elusive, mysterious, seeming to prefer to draw attention to others. Frederick Dale Bruner once called the Spirit "the shy member" of the Trinity. If we look to the Spirit, the Spirit defers, directing our attention to Jesus or to the Father to whom Jesus prayed. Mystics who have known the Spirit intimately have taught us that the Spirit is humble and modest, seeking no praise or adoration, but serving others, laying down her rights, serving us by enabling us to praise and adore Christ, to worship and serve God. Clark Pinnock captured this thought: "The Spirit does not wish to be focused upon but to remain anonymous, a servant. .... The Spirit of love effaces himself in order to bless others. The flame of love is humble. .... Like a mother in the service of life, the Spirit is disinterested and does not look to personal advantage."

Perhaps then the Spirit enables us to be humble, to serve, to efface ourselves, not looking to personal advantage. In short, the Holy Spirit stands in the background of our lives, yet never far away, always right over our shoulders, pointing us toward the grandeur of God and the story of Christ, nudging us lovingly to discover our lives in God's story. How do we grasp that story?

# THE INSPIRATION OF SCRIPTURE

*Come, Holy Spirit, Midwife to the Word.*

*You breathed; and the pages of the Bible stirred,*

*fluttered, flew, sang, winging us into God's story*

*that is the story of my life. Instruct, correct my mind;*

*inspire me through the Word You generously inspired. Amen.*

We speak of the Bible as being "inspired." Inspiration need not mean the Bible is the literal, dictated words of God. After all, the Bible is not the Quran (the Koran), which claims to be the actual words of God, repeated verbatim by Muhammad. The Bible claims to be human words about human interactions with God. Luke says he wanted to write about

Jesus, so he interviewed people and got the story down as best he could.

Not that this means the Bible is less authoritative, or less relevant. On the contrary, precisely because of the human element in Scripture, we discover in its pages an utterly realistic, believable, accessible story about God and human life, not someone else's long ago, but mine, yours, ours. The word "inspired" means "breathed in." The Holy Spirit, the living breath of God, breathed into these stories, poems, and letters the life of God so that the Bible might live with us, so that we might grasp the universe from God's perspective, so that we might read and understand what living with and for God is all about.

So inspiration isn't some radioactive property emanating from this book. Rather, inspiration is how God *uses* this book in our lives. Pay close attention to 2 Timothy 3:16: "All scripture is inspired by God and profitable for teaching, for reproof, for correction, and for training in righteousness, that [you] may be complete, equipped for every good work." If you imagine the Bible as inspired, then expect to be educated, reprimanded, disciplined, readied by the Spirit to charge out and do good in the world.

How generous of the Spirit, how fortunate for us, that the Spirit enabled people in biblical times to "get it" when God was acting before their eyes, that the Spirit motivated them to remember and to tell and retell the story, that the Spirit nudged somebody to write it all down, that the Spirit nagged editors to gather the writings onto longer scrolls, that the Spirit nursed the birthing of the collection of scrolls into what we think of as the Bible, that the Spirit prodded translators to render the Scriptures into modern languages, and many languages, so people like us could read, know, understand, wrestle, think, reflect, and discover God acting in our lives.

Martin Luther perceived a double kind of inspiration by which the Scriptures become a passable bridge into God's heart. The very Spirit that inspired the biblical writers is the same Spirit that inspires you and me when we read, when we listen. The Holy Spirit opens our minds, teaches us through the words on the page, leading us to understand and interpret what the Bible means today, here and now, for me, for us. The Holy Spirit rescues the Bible from the museum of religious relics and makes it real, vital today. And the Spirit does so not just by quickening our minds to understand, but by challenging us to quicken our steps, to get busy with our hands, to live out, to perform the Scriptures—or even to be laid aside for God's glory. When the Holy Spirit makes the Bible "happen" in what we as Christians do, and even simply in who we are, then we are the Body of Christ. For at the end of the day, what Scripture is about is Jesus.

# JESUS AND THE HOLY SPIRIT

*Come, Holy Spirit, bearer of Christ to the world:*

*You were with Jesus always, empowering, comforting,*

*fully intimate. You are with Jesus as I pray right now.*

*Usher Jesus out of the Scriptures and into my life*

*so I too may be with him and You always, intimately. Amen.*

Why did the Holy Spirit bother inspiring the Scriptures? What was the goal? Not just so we could have an admirable holy book to be proud of. The Spirit's purpose was that we might know Christ. Martin Luther once said that the Scriptures are "the swaddling clothes in which Christ is laid." Jesus himself, when debating the Pharisees who knew their Bibles backward and forward, said, "You search the scriptures, because you think that in them you have eternal life; and it is they that bear witness to me" (John 5:39).

If we want to know about the Spirit, we look to Jesus; if we want to know Jesus, we look to the Spirit. Jesus was on unusually intimate terms with the Spirit. Choose a single chapter, like Luke 4. "Jesus, full of the Holy Spirit . . . was led by the Spirit for forty days in the wilderness." Then "Jesus returned in the power of the Spirit into Galilee." He then went to Nazareth and spoke: "The Spirit of the Lord is upon me." As Clark Pinnock wrote, "The Gospels go out of the way to connect Jesus with the Spirit on all kinds of occasions in his life—birth, baptism, temptation, preaching, healing, exorcisms, death and resurrection. Overall they reveal Jesus as a gift of the Spirit."

Jesus is the gift of the Spirit. And the Holy Spirit is the one who snatches Jesus off the pages of once-upon-a-time history and makes Jesus very real and present today. The Spirit is the one who brings Jesus, who lived two thousand years ago, into the very room where you are reading this and penetrates your own heart, luring you toward Jesus, who cannot gather dust as some relic of the religious past, but embraces you by the Spirit in love, leading you on an adventure of faith and service to God.

Back in the second century, Irenaeus spoke of the double mission of the Son and the Spirit in this way: Jesus and the Holy Spirit are "the two hands of God," working in concert to touch, teach, heal, serve, and save. The challenge for us is: how can I know this Spirit? How can I be in touch with the Spirit? In a way, this is the wrong question, for the Spirit is already very much in touch with you. But we have a knack for closing our eyes, for running and hiding. What we desire, though, is to open ourselves to the Spirit. How does this opening happen?

---

# PRAYER AND THE SPIRIT

*Come Holy Spirit: teach us how to pray.*

*My prayer is feeble and confused. But I am praying,*

*and I thank You for this treasure of infinite value.*

*You are my sighing. Never stop whispering prayers,*

*too deep for words, out of the marrow of my soul. Amen.*

The Holy Spirit is prayer. Now, to diagram, to parse, to internalize this less-than-obvious sentence requires considerable dexterity. Isn't prayer something I choose to do? something I struggle to do? something I wish I did more, and better? and always something *I* do?

I was so encouraged the day I read Frederick Buechner's suggestion: "Everybody prays whether he thinks of it as praying or not. The odd silence you fall into when something very beautiful is happening or something very good or bad. The ah-h-h! that sometimes floats up out of you, the stammer of pain at somebody else's pain, the stammer of joy at somebody else's joy. Whatever words or sounds you use for sighing with over your own life. These are all prayers in their way. These are spoken not just to yourself but to something more familiar than yourself." Remember Paul's words? "Likewise the Spirit helps us in our weakness; for we do not know how to pray as we ought, but that very Spirit intercedes with sighs too deep for words. And God, who searches the heart, knows what is the mind of the Spirit, because the Spirit intercedes for the saints according to the will of God" (Romans 8:26-27 NRSV). If you are anxious about prayer, if you fear you will miss the Spirit, then relax: prayer is already happening. Prayer is going on all the time. When you weren't paying attention, when you weren't asking for it, the Spirit set up residence in your soul, helping you in your weakness, sighing and lifting up your every concern in prayer.

You do not need to create the possibility of contact with the Spirit. In fact, you cannot create that possibility. For the Holy Spirit is all gift, entirely free. And the gift of the Holy Spirit is none other than the Holy Spirit.

Knowing this, being grasped by this uninvited love, moves us to pray. The disciples pleaded with Jesus, "Lord, teach us to pray," and Jesus has given us the Spirit to draw us into prayer, to guide us through prayer, to make up for our deficits in prayer, to pray on our behalf when we simply cannot pray. Our challenge is to stop erecting walls that separate us from the Spirit.

So to know the Spirit, to have a lively sense of the Spirit, to be fundamentally altered by the Spirit, you must have what John Calvin called a "teachable spirit" (*docilitas* in Latin, whose cognate you may recognize—"docile"). Prayer, establishing a relationship with God, living the Christian life: This is not something *I* do. The smartest, the most agile person, the one with the grittiest determination, the spiritual giant—none of us are able to connect with

God. Paul's ominous warning, "Do not quench the Spirit" (1 Thessalonians 5:19), reminds us to stop erecting stupid walls of self-protection and spiritual grandeur.

Instead, we are humble, we are happily docile, nobly weak, and we discover the gift already given, the Holy Spirit, who is our relationship with God. Prayer entails a titanic struggle; we sag under the burden of combat, our only hope being that it is the Spirit who triumphs for us, through us. Any other approach to the Spirit is doomed to futility. Listen to Evelyn Underhill: "The Holy Spirit educates us in inner stillness, and it is for lack of this that most spiritual lives are so crude and shallow and vague." To enjoy a spiritual life that is not crude, shallow, or vague, we must first notice where exactly the Spirit is located.

# THE SPIRIT AND CREATION

*Come Holy Spirit, brood again over Your creation.*

*Open my eyes to notice the splendid tapestry of life;*

*open my ears to hear the sterling chorus of life,*

*as all things bear witness to Your goodness, power,*

*and glory. May I rest with the universe in your hands. Amen.*

At the moment time began, in the beginning, "the earth was without form and void, and darkness was upon the face of the deep; and the Spirit of God was moving over the face of the waters" (Genesis 1:2). Too often we think of the Holy Spirit as involved in the inner, pious life; and we forget that the Spirit is "the breath of life which causes all creation, all history, to flow together to its ultimate end, in the infinite ocean of God," as Pope John Paul II so beautifully described it. Where is the Spirit? Everywhere, before all things, above, under, permeating every living (and nonliving!) thing, between the lines of history, and most certainly beyond and after the time all things will be no more.

The Spirit wishes we would never underestimate the grandeur of God, never minimize the powerful tenderness of God, never miss out on the profligate creativity of God, whom we can imagine laughing in the divine laboratory, reveling in yet one more new-fangled form of life, this God who (as Annie Dillard put it) is "willing to try anything." To know the Spirit we look to creation, big and small. Listen to astronomers rattle off numbers measuring the expanse of the Milky Way, hundreds of thousands of light years, although our galaxy is a mere drop in an ocean measured in billions of light years. Recall that the pinholes of light we see in the night have been rushing toward us through nothing at all for millennia, all to be absorbed into microscopic fibers in the retina, nerves pulsating with the awestruck impression into the brain. God is glorified in the vastness of space, a glory mirrored in the minutiae of the inner workings of a cell, a glory resident in the space between nucleus and electron.

The Spirit's lavish production did not come about in a moment. John Polkinghorne wrote that the Creator "is not a God in a hurry; rather God is patient and subtle in relation to a world that its Creator has allowed largely to 'make itself.' There is unlikely to be any other way in which love would choose to work." And the Spirit did not wind up the universe like an old mechanical clock to be left ticking. The same Spirit that brooded over the waters in Genesis continues to brood over streams, forests, everglades, paved cities, through windows, burrowing down deep into the depths of the earth and of my soul, and yours too. To honor the Spirit, we reverence the work of the Spirit. We weep when some species becomes extinct, for one more voice in the great chorus of creation's praise has been silenced.

The Spirit is everywhere, and it is our pleasure to be alert to signs of the Spirit's ongoing labor. Annie Dillard has helped many of us by spending time outside, noticing aphids, barnacles, hummingbirds, and rocks, and rightly she suggests that "the least we can do is notice." A friend of mine who is an astronomer once invited me to look through his telescope at the moons of Saturn, which he knew were in some unusual alignment. He said, "Do you know why I love these moments? It makes me feel at home."

By the Spirit who is love, we are at home, utterly dependent upon the Spirit who is never here and not there, but is never far from us. Listen to Job 34:14:

"If [God] should take back his spirit to himself,
    and gather to himself his breath,
all flesh would perish together,
    and man would return to dust."

For every breath we take, we are grateful to the Holy Spirit.

# THE SPIRIT IN US

*Come, Holy Spirit, breathe into me Your life.*

*Blow deep within my soul, turn my life inside out.*

*Catch me up in the powerful vortex of Your gale,*

*for only You can use my restlessness to bring calm.*

*I long to live in the eye of the hurricane of Your love. Amen.*

Is the Holy Spirit in me? We must knead our language carefully here. While we may speak of my having the Spirit in me, or in us, the divine person who is the Holy Spirit is utterly uncontainable inside me. The Spirit is too big, too wild, too grandiose, to talk about it in any way that even hints that the Spirit is something I have got. My fondest dream is not that I will ever have the Spirit in me, but rather that I will be swept up in the whirlwind of the Spirit.

In the Garden of Eden, God breathed this life-giving wind, this Spirit, into Adam and Eve (Genesis 2:7). In a locked room, Jesus appeared to his disciples after the resurrection and "breathed" his Spirit on them (John 20:22). My daughter's birth announcement was taken from Psalm 139: "For you formed my inward parts, you knit me together in my mother's womb. Wonderful are your works! For my frame was not hidden from you, when I was being made in secret. Your eyes beheld my unformed substance." Her name is Grace, and her life, and my life, is all grace. The life of the Spirit, for which we are desperately thirsty, isn't in me but is everything to me. We "receive" the Spirit (Acts 8:15-17), but we never own it. My life, my purpose, my continuing to live, my getting any place that matters—all this is a gift, all grace.

So we need not be surprised that the faithful have so often spoken of having the Spirit "in me." For the Spirit works from the inside out, uprooting our errant desires and impulses, replacing them with the Spirit's fruit, so that our inner selves are so transparent to the movement of the Spirit that we would not wish to find any knot inside us that is not given over to the Spirit's pervasive presence. When we approach the Lord's table, we take into our mouths the body and blood of Christ in a marvelous feast of the Spirit's getting at us from the inside, living as our heavenly sustenance.

As soon as the species *homo sapiens* first stood up and used its large, complex brain, its peculiar soul, some kind of spirituality existed. We are made to be spiritual; we are spiritual. The Spirit causes me to be spiritual. The Spirit is not my spirituality, but the Spirit awakens my consciousness of God. The Spirit opens my mind and soul up to God. The Spirit lures me, lures us toward God. The Spirit actually burrows into our soul and makes our hearts restless, so we will experience (with St. Augustine) that "You have made us for yourself, O Lord, and our hearts are restless until they find rest in you." Restlessness: We know it so very well, the dissatisfaction in which we meander, the way we ricochet from one diversion to the next, always peering around the next corner, forgetting what it would feel like to be at home. Restlessness: Is it a curse? or a gift? Perhaps the fog would lift if we quite simply decided to think of our restlessness as woven into our souls by a loving Holy Spirit who knew we would need some inner ache to draw us toward our true home.

## LESSON TEN

# THE SPIRIT AND FEELING

*Come, Holy Spirit, Master of the interior life:*

*My combustible feelings at times are sheer delight,*

*but then they cruelly turn on me, unraveling me.*

*Because You are beyond mere feeling, You are the one*

*who can heal, refine, and stir my deepest feelings. Amen.*

Regularly I hear from people who are giving up on God and their faith because "I just don't feel what I think I am supposed to feel." When did feelings become the litmus test of whether the Spirit is a reality? or even whether our faith in God is meaningful? Jesus came into the world, not so we might feel different but so we could be different.

So we are wise to avoid identifying the Spirit with warm fuzzy feelings about God. The feelings I have are as peculiar to me as my fingerprint; they are like untamable creatures in the wild—fascinating, dangerous, hard to get a handle on. We cannot make interior emotions the litmus test for the Spirit. The Holy Spirit is with me and you always, whether we feel it or know it or not. Martin Luther worried that the tumult of spiritual feeling can actually be the work of the devil, who hopes that we will give up on God once we find ourselves in a dry, barren desert of emotion. Perhaps Evelyn Underhill put it best: Feelings are "the chocolate creams of the Christian life. It is by no means always the perfect lovers who have such feelings. Do not make the mistake of thinking, if you sometimes feel cold and dead, that you do not know how to love."

Mind you, the Holy Spirit knows how to love; and one marvelous, unexpectedly titillating gift of the Spirit's love is that elusive, intimate, profoundly delicious, soaringly beautiful feeling that occasionally comes when we yield ourselves to God. Such a feeling is a gift we cannot demand, but can only relish, remember, and relate. If you long for the Spirit to become more evident, you should spend time listening to God's friends talking about their experiences of the Spirit, even sidling up next to them in the pew or at the prayer rail. Ecstasy, the miracle of the Spirit lifting us up and out of our selves, happens, and can move those open to the Spirit not merely to experience the Spirit but to embody a changed life.

The Spirit not only grants a few precious moments of such ecstasy. The Spirit also takes other feelings resident in our souls and brings healing. Our feelings are wrapped up in the Spirit's loving embrace, and they can be healed and transformed. Feelings of grief, feelings of anger, feelings of unworthiness, feelings of vengeance, feelings of disappointment—all these are borne by the Spirit and can be transformed, repaired, even washed away by the Spirit who created the universe and can handle our emotions.

Yet we need to recognize that the Spirit engages in other labors over our feelings, and the results may seem exceedingly unpleasant. The curious gift of restlessness is but one. A second is the aftermath of the Spirit wielding its scalpel within our lost, wayward souls, causing us pain, humiliation, even embarrassment when we are convicted of sin.

# THE CONVICTION OF SIN

*Come, Holy Spirit, from whom nothing is hidden:*

*Expose me, search every dark corner of my soul.*

*You love me too much to flatter me; You are my friend.*

*Your sorrow over my sin lures me into confession;*

*Your loving judgment is my only hope of ever being clean. Amen.*

Paul reminds us that the Spirit "searches everything" (1 Corinthians 2:10), and we may wish the Spirit were not quite so nosy. The Holy Spirit has the rude, impolite task of convicting us of sin. And the Spirit is thorough in this unwelcome labor, casting her searchlight not just on our big, obvious sins but on small, subtle, seemingly trivial ways in which we rebel against God, hidden sins, even unintentional sins. The Spirit fingers some dark corner of my soul, and I cry out defensively, "But I never thought about that!" And the Spirit bows before the glory of new truth coming out of the closet.

How relentless is the Spirit? Read Jesus' words in Matthew 5. Never dare to say "I am not guilty of murder, or adultery," for at the heart of murder and adultery are anger and lust. Picky, picky, this probing, humbling, searching Spirit.

Notice that the Spirit's work in convicting us of sin is not the same as "conscience." Many of us believe we have some inner, built-in moral equipment. We do, but we need to consider its origin. From parents, teachers, and now the media, we accrue a massive collection of little recorded messages in our heads which say "okay" or "whoa!" But we can never trust this random assortment of messages. The Holy Spirit's work is greater, truer, less prone to error, than what even the noblest parents and friends might plant in our minds. The Spirit is always outside us, never just inside us, and so we are not the owners of our own moral checks and balances. We are judged by one outside ourselves. I am judged, my behaviors, my thoughts, even my "conscience"—all are judged by the Spirit.

But this convicting work is nothing but love. Aristotle said that the opposite of a friend is a flatterer. The Holy Spirit never flatters us. The Spirit loves us too much for that. The Spirit is my friend, wanting the best for me, knowing that only the truth will set me free. The Spirit's passion is for us to love the true God and to lead true lives, growing ever closer into holiness, fleeing from the tempters who glitter but are most assuredly not gold. Our prayer may be these words from Andrew Reed's hymn:

Holy Spirit, all divine,
Dwell within this heart of mine,

Cast down every idol throne,
Reign supreme, and reign alone.

The Spirit not only exposes our sin. The Spirit weeps, grieving over our sinfulness (Ephesians 4:30). These beloved tears of the Spirit inform all that the Spirit yearns to do with us next, for the Spirit could never stop at merely pointing the finger. The Spirit begins a long, loving labor of changing us, purifying us, altering us. Indeed, the Spirit is "a consuming fire" (Hebrews 12:29), purging all that is unholy. And we must not shrink from that fire, but join forces; for Evelyn Underhill was right: "The Holy Spirit isn't like one of those patented cleansers that does our washing while we are asleep! It works through our brave and willing cooperation, our active use of all the material we are offered, even everything that damages our vanity and opposes our self-will." What does the Spirit do with our will?

# THE SPIRIT AND SANCTIFICATION

*Come, Holy Spirit; Your holiness is beautiful to me.*

*I want to be holy, but am embarrassingly unable to climb*

*out of that awful hole my rebel lifestyle has dug.*

*Create in me a clean heart; plant Your life in my life*

*so I may discover Your fruit prospering even in me. Amen.*

Y ou shall be holy, for I the LORD your God am holy"
(Leviticus 19:2). God bridges the impassable chasm
between us and God, a gulf burrowed out by our
crazed rebellion, our lack of goodness, our unholy, sinful
existence, so immeasurably far are we from the utter goodness, holiness, and purity of God. This bridge across is the
Holy Spirit.

Charles Wesley penned a hymn which prays,

> Deepen the wound thy hands have made
> In this weak, helpless soul,
> Till mercy, with its balmy aid,
> Descends to make me whole.

Or as children sing at Christmas,

> Be near me, Lord Jesus, I ask thee to stay
> close by me forever, and love me, I pray;
> bless all the dear children in thy tender care,
> and fit us for heaven to live with thee there.

The Spirit's merciful, kindly intention is to make us fit for God.

Theologians have spoken of a doctrine called "sanctification." "Justification" (our salvation) is what God has done *for* us. "Sanctification" (meaning "made holy") is what God does *in* us. Gordon Fee claims that "for Paul there is no such thing as 'salvation in Christ' that does not also include righteousness on the part of God's people ... because both 'getting in' and 'staying in' are the work of the Spirit."

Holiness is not a matter of gritting our teeth and trying really diligently to do what God requires. We may grit our teeth, and we do try hard. But I am not able to do what God wants of me, I am not capable of the life God wants for me. A changed life is the gift of God's Spirit. As a humble believer, I know that any good that I manage is "not I, but Christ in me" (from Galatians 2:20). The Spirit gets up in the morning and hounds us, pursuing a changed life, what Fee called "the reproduction of the life of Christ in the believer." Paul described this new life, the life for which we were made, the only life that will ever satisfy us, as "the fruit of the Spirit." Not "the fruit of my good intentions," but "the fruit of the Spirit": "love, joy, peace, patience, kindness, goodness, faithfulness, gentleness, self-control. Against such there is no law" (from Galatians 5:22-23).

Not only are these not against the law. They are not the law! Paul does not say, "You must be joyful, patient, faithful." Rather, if we just calm down and let the Spirit have its way with us, we discover to our delightful surprise traces of joy, peace, gentleness in our lives, all gift, all the work of God in us.

Why should it matter if we are sanctified? Because in creation, God made us, you and me, in God's own image. We are the image of God, we are the way God is imaged in this world, and so we must be holy. Paul said that my body is the "temple of the Holy Spirit" (1 Corinthians 6:19). How humbling! How fearsome! How manifestly impossible it is for me to be anything like the kind of temple our splendidly wonderful God would need! And yet I am to be, you are to be this temple. St. Basil said it is "the Lord who commands ... the Spirit who strengthens. What kind of strengthening is this? Perfection in holiness, which expresses itself in an unyielding, unchangeable commitment to goodness. Such holiness is impossible without the Spirit." And such holiness is exceedingly difficult in our culture.

# Culture and the Spirit

*Come, Holy Spirit, Stranger to this unholy world:*

*Heighten my discomfort, and sharpen my alienation*

*so I may scorn the dazzling sights that would blind me*

*to Your lovely light. Shove me, nip at my heels*

*so I will run toward the truth that makes me odd. Amen.*

Christians who would be holy must cultivate a sense of living as aliens in a foreign land or on some strange planet. We can affirm the goodness of God's creation, but the world is fallen; and life as we experience it does not mirror the glory of God. To know the Spirit, to be awakened to living in the Spirit, you must be vigilant and forever suspicious about the bogus values of the culture in which we find ourselves. The Spirit's work is not to help us fit in to this world. The Spirit's work is not to assist our quest for the rewards this world has to offer. The Spirit sets us at odds with this world, whose sights and sounds dazzle and titillate; so we had better keep our distance from a culture that will engulf and drown us. Our culture prizes competitiveness, achievement, efficiency, looking out for number one, getting ahead, looking fantastic, being cool. This culture mandates that any desire you happen to feel simply must be satisfied. Everything is about self-interest; we have even heard that going to church or serving the needy "makes me feel good." But "the fruit of the Spirit is love" (Galatians 5:22), and love is the antithesis of self-absorption. Love is giving myself away, focusing on someone else. Some tornado must whip through our souls to break us loose from our curved-in self-concern and cast us out of ourselves into loving.

Paul lists "love" as the first "fruit of the Spirit," and Philip Kenneson has written that the eight others (joy, peace, patience, kindness, goodness, faithfulness, gentleness, self-control) "might best be understood as amplifying and further specifying what is entailed by this way of love. In short, these other eight dispositions, taken together, characterize a life lived in, by and through God's love. In this sense, love is much like light, which, when passing through a prism, breaks into its component colors." How lovely, this colorful life of love.

But how uncolorful, how bizarre, how boring this life will seem to those immersed in our culture. Paul's prism of the fruit of the Spirit will appear to be a mere chunk of old glass to a world that gawks after its own list of pursuits. Think about the seven deadly sins: greed, lust, gluttony, pride, envy, anger, and sloth, which the Church for centuries warned us about. These now describe the "good life" in America. Movies, television, sports, politics, and conversation are all about greed, lust, gluttony, pride, envy, anger, and sloth. Children grow up eager to master all seven under the tutelage of the mass media.

The media's darlings work overtime to manufacture ever new desires in our souls. What could be more inimical to life in the Spirit than watching a round of television commercials? We must shop, we must produce, we must hurry, we must be tough, we must fit in. Little wonder the Spirit seems so vague and distant. For we are consumed with consuming, while the Spirit is standing outside the marketplace crying over the racket, "Run for your life!" Daniel 3 tells a story we dare not leave for children only: Shadrach, Meshach, and Abednego refrain from the imperial diet, they refuse to bow down to the king's idol, they courageously stick out as weirdos who cannot be bullied into fitting in to a culture not of God. In a rage, Nebuchadnezzar hurls them into the fiery furnace. How could he have known that the true God is on friendly terms with fire, that the Spirit is a fire? In the fire of the distinctive life, God is found, a God who is not so small as our petty self-interest, but a God larger than the infinite expanse of the universe itself.

# THE SPIRIT AS CREATOR

*Come, Holy Spirit, Architect of all creation:*

*You bring order out of chaos, inexorably yet surely,*

*weaving beauty and goodness through all things*

*living and inanimate. With them I praise You and pray*

*that You refashion the world You once fashioned. Amen.*

Beginning in the beginning with Genesis, the Spirit broods over the formless void and brings order out of the chaos, creating, vivifying, nurturing universe, world, life. Hildegard of Bingen extolled the Spirit in poetry:

> The Holy Spirit is life-giving life,
> Universal Mover and the root of all creation,
> refiner of all things from their dross,
> brings forgiveness of guilt and oil for our wounds,

is radiance of life, most worthy of worship,
wakening and reawakening both earth and heaven.

Of course, to the modern mind, very different competitors attempt to explain why things are the way they are. Scientists, many of whom are brilliant (or even witty, if we read Richard Dawkins or Stephen Jay Gould), argue for a randomness, that energies and forces happened, that life just emerged, that the fittest do manage over the millennia to get ahead. They detect no "spirit" with their equipment. The Spirit is not terribly offended by this viewpoint, for the Spirit delights in anonymity, working behind the scenes, even bringing beauty and goodness out of processes that scientists in many ways understand better than theologians. The spirit's work in creation benefits the loudly raging atheist as well as the humbly pious believer. The Spirit is pleased when children study science and when adults continue to gaze up into the skies at light whose age is in the millions, when we explore the inner minutiae of nature; for over time the more we learn about all the Spirit has caused to exist, the more we will understand the Spirit, and (if we refuse to let steel encase our souls) the more we will know and love God the Creator and God's son, Jesus. The Spirit, after all, longed to fashion a theater in which God could be glorified, a stage on which Jesus could walk, and so over a dozen billion years "Creation unfolded under the presidency of the Holy Spirit" (Pinnock).

Creation may be analyzed; Creation then is to praised in song. Throughout the psalms, in hymnody, in poetry, the Spirit inspires tunes and words so we might declare the wonder of the very creation that same Spirit nursed to life. And there is a lovely thread woven through Creation: hope. For if the Spirit created and nurtures all things, then we may always count on the Spirit to cope creatively with disruption, with disorder, with every kind of disaster. The Spirit renews, re-creates (Psalm 104:30), recovering God's initial but squandered intention for us. Jesus said to

Nicodemus, "Do not marvel that I said to you, 'You must be born anew.' The [Spirit] blows where it wills, and you hear the sound of it, but you do not know whence it comes or whither it goes; so it is with every one who is born of the Spirit" (John 3:7-8). But before we say more about the personal effects of the Spirit, we need to say one more thing about the Spirit's world in which we find ourselves.

# HISTORY AND THE SPIRIT

*Come, Holy Spirit, Lord over all history:*

*All worldly kingdoms are mere pretenders.*

*You are the author of the true (if hidden) history*

*of our world, Your world, which cannot stray too far*

*from Your eternal purpose, in which I trust. Amen.*

When we live openly with the Holy Spirit, our souls are stretched outward by some centrifugal force, and the Spirit cultivates in our hearts a passion about the larger world, the past, and the future of the world. The psalmist asks, "Why do the nations [rage]?... He who sits in the heavens laughs" (Psalm 2:1, 4). The sweeping events of history have often frightened the people of God. We are overwhelmed to contemplate the litany of powers, the Babylonians, Pharaohs, Alexander the Great, Caesar Augustus, Visigoths and Huns, Genghis Khan, Napoleon, Nazis, Stalin, even America, and more recently terrorists with no nationality at all. Powers rage across the earth and seem to mock the notion that there is a God at all.

But the Spirit that brooded over creation is subtly, invisibly, but relentlessly interweaving another plot (not detectable by the naked eye) through the story of humanity. The Spirit laughs over the great powers, admittedly after a flood of tears. For all the powers ultimately collapse under their own ponderous weight, demonstrating that no earthly power is absolute. The Spirit is forever exposing the truth about the inevitable corruption of the powers. The Spirit is whispering in minds, changing hearts, never throwing in the towel, so that Karl Heim's lovely verdict always comes to pass: "God sets up his throne on the wreckage of human earthly thrones, and the history of the world is strewn with the wreckage of demolished imperialisms and smashed altars, whose debris reveals impressively the sole Lordship of God."

Human history, the plot for all people, took a definitive turn when God pledged, "I will pour out my Spirit upon all flesh" (Joel 2:28, Acts 2:17). There is no longer Jew or Gentile (Galatians 3:28), for the Spirit gathers all people, without distinction, into God's plan of salvation. Distinctions and divisions are of sinful human devising, and the Spirit is a zealous wrecking ball, crashing down every wall; for because of the Spirit we are one, not two or seventy or a million.

History is not manipulated by divine decree. But history is not random. The Spirit, patiently over a few million years, is bringing creation to its happy conclusion. My life and the life of the Church, therefore, are neither fixed by decree nor a random succession of happenstances. The same Spirit patiently embracing the history of the world patiently embraces me and my history. The Holy Spirit does not swoop down for me and mine whenever I summon her, but catches me up into the broader adventure of what God is inexorably doing in the world, through time. The part I play may be small, but I am playing a part; for I too am not the center of things. Reinhold Niebuhr wrote, "Nothing worth doing can be accomplished in a single lifetime." What the Spirit leads me to do in my lifetime is a mere step in the Spirit's march through history, one I am privileged to take.

And I do not take that step alone. The Spirit draws me into the Church, which has its own history. The British novelist (and close friend of C. S. Lewis) Charles Williams wrote a history of Christendom and entitled it *The Descent of the Dove*. The Spirit has birthed all that is good about the Church, and the same Spirit has borne patiently the trifling stupidity of the Church. The Spirit kneads both the wondrous glory of the Church and the embarrassing floundering of the Church together, and we have a feeble yet curiously beautiful witness to the Spirit; for my life with the Spirit is lived out with other Christians in the Church or not at all.

# THE SPIRIT IN THE CHURCH

*Come, Holy Spirit, our perpetual Pentecost:*

*You gave birth to the Church, which is not ours,*

*but Yours, even in our bumbling foolhardiness.*

*Come mightily upon Your Church once more,*

*and knit me into the glorious fabric of the saints. Amen.*

Perhaps we should say "The Church in the Holy Spirit." The church (whether we are thinking of a physical cathedral or wooden A-frame, or of the gathered people of God) never contains or possesses the Spirit. Hopefully the Spirit possesses us, rests upon us, ignites us and catapults us out into the world to be about God's purposes. We say the Church was "born" at Pentecost (Acts 2), when the Spirit caught everyone by surprise, rifling through the upper room like wind, or fire, some tornado of white hot heat; and the Church's first moment of existence was not a still life, pastel figures posing serenely in prayer. Instead, the Church's first moment was a rushing, people flying out of the exits, speaking words they hadn't known five minutes before, hell-bent on grabbing the next person in the marketplace and hugging them with a transforming word about Jesus.

Or was the Church born when the risen Jesus mysteriously stood in front of dejected disciples who didn't think they had let him in the door—and he "breathed" on them (John 20:22)? Or was the Church born at an earlier Pentecost centuries before when the Israelites cowered beneath the thundering blaze on Mt. Sinai; Moses read them the commandments, and with sheer joy the people declared "All that the LORD has commanded we will do" (from Exodus 24:3), launching a radically different kind of community that lived intimately with God, the very people from whom Jesus came?

Blushing, we have to admit that the Church stupidly loses its way. Frederick Buechner wryly suggested that "the best thing that could happen to the church would be for some great tidal wave of history to wash all that away—the church buildings tumbling, the church money all lost, the church bulletins blowing through the air like dead leaves, the differences between preachers and congregations all lost too. Then all we would have left would be each other and Christ, which was all there was in the first place."

But can't the buildings and money bear holy witness to God, as even a gaudy steeple declares to a surrounding village, "There is still a God"? The bulletins? They usually bear small words that are the mighty work of the Holy Spirit, like "Pray for Myrtle Davis, who is in Memorial Hospital," or "Come to the BBQ to raise money for choir robes," or "John Bolton's funeral will be tomorrow at 2:00."

Such is the life of the people of God, simple, mundane, tender, with trivial yet palpable embodiments of the life of the Holy Spirit.

For we are saved by God not so "I can have a personal relationship with God." That personal relationship isn't like having a personal trainer or a personal tailor. I have the same savior as everybody else, and I am saved in order to be saved with you, all of us together. When we praise God in eternity, I will not sing solo, and neither shall you; we will join a mighty chorus, each voice contributing—yet lost in the wonder, love, and praise of the great throng of the communion of the saints. When we praise God today in worship, we enjoy one of the Spirit's most lovely gifts.

# WORSHIP IN THE SPIRIT

*Come, Holy Spirit, reveal Yourself in worship,*

*for we long to experience You in Your sanctuary,*

*so we may reconize You more clearly in the world.*

*Hush us when we kneel, thrill us when we sing,*

*unclog our ears so we may taste and see Your goodness. Amen.*

Choirs once summoned us to worship by intoning, "The Lord is in his holy temple, let all the earth keep silence before him." The Spirit sets up residence in the sanctuary, which need not imply the Spirit somehow is inside the church but not outside. Rather, the same Spirit from which you cannot flee in your most heathen-stricken moments, the same Spirit which lurks around every corner and across every square inch of earth—this Spirit longs for a special time of meeting with us in worship, precisely so we will recover our ability to notice the Spirit when we are not in worship.

We look closely for the Spirit's movement within worship. The hymns are transformed, no longer little religious songs but a chorus of praise in union with the saints in every place and age. Prayers ripple outward, gathered up with every other worshiper awestruck by the privilege of being heard by the God of the universe. Annie Dillard tells of attending a church on Puget Sound where one Sunday the priest interrupted his supplications, looked up toward the ceiling, and cried out in some strangely hopeful exasperation, "Lord, we bring you these same petitions every week!" And then he continued. The Spirit is in the regularity, the repetition of our praying, as we make repentance, supplication, thanksgiving as routine as breathing. For the Spirit is wonderfully routine, and at the same time never merely routine. The Spirit erupts and interrupts and surprises in worship: an unforeseen tear, an unanticipated *ahhh*, truth sneaking up behind us when we aren't looking and jolting us into some new life we weren't looking for.

The sermon is a busy moment for the Spirit. On Tuesday that Spirit was whispering ideas into the preacher's ear in the study and now lifts the heads of worshipers to hear that Word, to answer again James Weldon Johnson's prayer for the preacher:

O Lord, we come this morning . . .
Like empty pitchers to a full fountain, . . .
And now, O Lord, this man of God,
Who breaks the bread of life this morning—
Shadow him in the hollow of thy hand,
And keep him out of the gunshot of the devil.
Take him, Lord—this morning—
Wash him with hysop inside and out,
Hang him up and drain him dry of sin.
Pin his ear to the wisdom-post,
And make his words sledge hammers of truth . . .
Put his eye to the telescope of eternity, . . .
Put perpetual motion in his arms,

Fill him full of the dynamite of thy power,
Anoint him all over with the oil of thy salvation,
And set his tongue on fire.

As is no doubt the case when we pray together, the
Spirit's best work happens in worship when we are silent,
in those lingering moments between sentences, during that
pregnant pause, as the Spirit takes the preacher's paltry
words, just as the Spirit takes the prayer's feeble pleas, and
ennobles them with grace and hope.

Nowhere is the Spirit more palpable than in the
Sacraments. Hidden in the waters of baptism is the invig-
orating gift of the Spirit. We are baptized with water; we are
baptized with the Spirit. The Spirit washes us, cleanses us.
The Spirit refreshes us, quenching our thirst. The Spirit
draws us into the great stream, the deep river of God's people in every time and place.

At times, our response to the bestowal of the Spirit in
baptism is tepid; and so to keep our life with God revital-
ized, we gather at the Lord's table, where it is the Spirit
whose delight is in our fellowship with the Lord and each
other. The priest prays, "Pour out your Holy Spirit on us
gathered here, and on these gifts of bread and wine." We
gather as the Body of Christ, and the Spirit then transforms
us into the Body of Christ.

We may revel in St. Ephrem's prayer:

In Your Bread, Lord, there is hidden the Spirit who
is not consumed,
in Your Wine there dwells the Fire that is not drunk:
the Spirit is in Your Bread, the Fire in Your Wine,
a manifest wonder, that our lips have received,
And that worship is our work in the world.

Yet nowhere does the Spirit show off her creativity so
much as in worship, and so we pause for a moment to consider the Spirit and Pentecostalism.

# THE EXPERIENCE OF PENTECOSTALISM

*Come, Holy Spirit, ever full of surprises:*

*Thank You for this movement, Pentecostalism;*

*for without it we might wonder if You were slumbering.*

*Rush upon us, ravish us, loosen my tongue, let her speak*

*in words new, strange, evocative, beautiful—and true. Amen.*

The twentieth century was jolted by a vibrant movement within a church grown stodgy. An Episcopal rector told his congregation he had been filled by the Spirit and had spoken in tongues. The bishop (laughably) banned speaking in tongues—as if the Spirit could be legislated! Frank Bartleman tells what happened to him at the Azusa Street mission in Los Angeles and subsequent experiences:

The Spirit came mightily upon ... the whole company ... for three hours.... Men would fall all over the house, like the slain in battle, or rush for the altar.... The scene often resembled a forest of fallen trees.... All at once I seemed to hear in my soul ... a rich voice speaking in a language I did not know.... It seemed to ravish and fully satisfy the pent up praises in my being.... I was fully yielded to God, simply carried by his will, as on a divine stream.... A heaven of conscious bliss accompanied it.... My body began to rock and I fell over onto the piano and lay there. It was a cyclonic manifestation of the power of God.... This opened the channel for a new ministry of the Spirit in service.... The Spirit began to flow through me in a new way. Messages would come, with anointings.... The Pentecostal baptism spells complete abandonment, possession by the Holy Ghost, ... with a spirit of instant obedience. The early church lived in this, as its normal atmosphere.... Wiseacres cannot reach this. Oh, to become a fool.... Newspapers began to ridicule and abuse the meetings. The devil overdid himself again. Outside persecution never hurt the work.

Across denominational boundaries, among the poor of Latin America and Africa, yet also among the educated and affluent of America, the Spirit ignited long-forgotten phenomena, like tongues, like ecstasy in worship, prophesying, signs and wonders, "spiritual gifts" (*charismata* in Greek), almost as if the Church was here and there remembering to be itself, the Spirit fanning once again the flames of Pentecost and the early church.

What rocked those first Christians so powerfully? Demons were exorcised, the sick were healed, singing was rhapsodic, utterance was inspired, prophesies by men and women were believed, the needy were served, and the speaking in tongues.... The wildness and unpredictability of the Spirit's movement is one of the ways God challenges our habitual efforts to be in control of our lives. The Spirit blows wherever it wishes.

Sadly, the Spirit's heart is repeatedly broken when Christians, zealous to possess the gifts of the Spirit, turn these charismatic wonders into sources of division and contention. The Spirit is more generous than we, embracing a wide family of believers, working not in a single way, but in multifarious ways among various Christian bodies. We are, after all, the Body of Christ, needing each other. Members of mainline denominations who are stiffly fixed in our pews need a little liberation from the Pentecostals so we too can move and show a little emotion. Pentecostals, at the same time, may benefit from a deeper rooting in the rich soil of Christian tradition. Together we adore the Spirit's work, which draws us together, deftly weaving the most mind-boggling experience together with the calm knowledge that our faith has a content that tests and grounds every experience.

Wherever and however we worship, the Holy Spirit is reluctant to let us leave the place at the end of worship, so she trails us out the door as a sweet memory, as a nagging reminder; for the Spirit's dream is to lure us into being not just hearers but "doers of the word" (James 1:22). That doing seems compromised at times, as Christians struggle to get on the same page.

# UNITY IN THE SPIRIT

*Come, Holy Spirit, for we are a fractured people.*

*Where divisions are sinful, judge, forgive, change us.*

*Where differences are unique gifts from You, use us*

*toward that great end when we finally sing,*

*"We are one in the Spirit, we are one in the Lord." Amen.*

C yril of Alexandria wrote, "All of us who have received the Holy Spirit are merged together with one another, and with God." It is one thing to talk about the Spirit achieving unity between God and myself. It is quite another to talk about the Spirit achieving unity between you and me, or among Christians. Paul mysteriously believes we are all one in Christ, and begs us "to maintain the unity of the Spirit in the bond of peace. There is one body and one Spirit, ... one hope, ... one Lord, one faith, one baptism" (Ephesians 4:3-5). We cannot see the Spirit, so we must imagine her face. Surely she shakes her head, wiping back weary tears, as she overhears staunch believers in Jesus expending their limited energies competing with each other, judging one another, like bickering juvenile siblings wasting their childhood sitting and pouting in the corner.

Or is there some sly grin on her face, as she takes the long, hidden view? Is God's love so all-enveloping that we nonetheless are one whether we like it or not, whether we've moved one inch toward one another or not? Are our differences precisely the bizarre design of the Spirit, not so we might bicker or splinter off but so real people, in all their startling diversity and uniqueness, might find a place in Christ's body? Division within the Church is evil in a way, but then God may use our division, as each denominational body has a special angle on the multifaceted orb that is the kingdom of God. One group is riveted on the Bible, another on serving the poor, another on liturgy, another on ecstasy. Together we are not a many-headed monster, but a body, reaching out to all kinds of people, accomplishing together unfathomably good things we could never manage alone.

So my church around the corner is a part of the Church universal. We worship in concert with the church in England, Lithuania, Kenya, Sri Lanka, and Taiwan. And we worship in concert with Abraham and Sarah, Moses and Miriam, Isaiah, Esther, Mary and Joseph, Peter and John, martyrs, saints, grandparents, and friends through the ages. This is the miracle of the Holy Spirit.

The Spirit draws us in, making us "members" of a church. Body parts are not all identical, but are certainly complementary. As C. S. Lewis put it, church members are not identically dressed and trained soldiers standing shoulder to shoulder. We vary as wildly as God's imagination. Yet the Spirit ensures we are a fellowship, a unity of which we are incapable, but of which the Spirit is surely capable. And the Spirit ensures that each of us is gifted for our very specialized place within the Body of Christ.

# DISCOVERING YOUR CALLING

*Come, Holy Spirit; I stop, gaze in the mirror,*

*and discover Your peculiar handiwork: me.*

*My life belongs to You. Spark my imagination,*

*prod my stubbornness, reveal my gifts (and wounds)*

*so when You call, I will follow You passionately. Amen.*

The Holy Spirit must have terrific fun while working in that secret factory where people are created, smiling over yet one more unique individual, creasing each fingerprint at a never before seen curvature, devising a maddeningly new personality, even between so-called identical twins. A passion for Mozart, mixed in with a head for numbers, sobered by a mental block with foreign languages, yet a flair for pastry crusts, a smile no one has ever anticipated, laughably surprising permutations, the Spirit strewing gifts and talents all over like that sower Jesus told us about (Mark 4). Whenever we notice whatever is good in me, in you, in any and all people, we witness the clever planning of the Holy Spirit. And if we want to be close to God, if we crave fulfillment in life, then we must first look to whatever little or big skill we have, lift our heads in gratitude to the Spirit, and then confess "My life is not my own. Use me as you will." The gifts the Spirit yearns to have at her disposal may be something as grand as Millard Fuller figuring out how to build Habitat homes around the world for the working poor, or something just as precious as my Aunt Zonia wiping my feverish forehead with a cool cloth.

Failure to let the Spirit use the Spirit's own gifts in you is futility, for to kick against the Spirit's continuous pressing is unwitting misery. When we let ourselves be used by the Spirit, surprises are in store. Jürgen Moltmann writes that believers "put their natural gifts and powers at the service of the congregation. But in the service of the congregation they make out of their gifts something different from what they were in other contexts." And then "new powers develop in them, powers which they were unaware of previously."

Sometimes the world has tried to extinguish our God-given fire, through the grind of daily drudgery, a brutal boss, or before a cold parent, as the devil never grows weary in his routine or of whispering negatives in the ears of God's precious children. Like many Christian heroes of centuries gone by, we may have to get rude when those whisperings come and shout at the darkness "I am gifted by the Holy Spirit. Yes, even me!"

Yet the most profound miracle of the Holy Spirit is not when I hand over my resumé of skills to the Lord. The most beautiful work of the Spirit comes when I dare to let my armor be ripped off, exposing the depths of my soul, where there are wounds. If you want to be close to God, if you want to find fulfillment and serve God, do not look just to your abilities. Look to the place inside where you have been wounded. In that wounded place, you will find the Holy Spirit. Do not be afraid of your brokenness, for cracks let the light in, or as Hemingway put it, "The world breaks everyone, and then some become strong in the broken places." In your broken places, you will discover the most lovely giftedness. In your broken places, you will meet the brokenness of others; and you will be able to touch them because you know, you remember. It's all about finding and living as near as possible to that intersection between your passion and what God is doing in the world. For at that junction, we look up and are startled to realize how very close we are to God.

# INTIMACY WITH GOD

*Come, Holy Spirit, bear witness in my soul,*

*that I discover myself cradled intimately by You.*

*Move me to cry, "Abba!"—absolutely assured*

*that I am heard, loved, tenderly and strongly.*

*Let me suffer with You, for I desire nothing besides You. Amen.*

Saint Basil wrote quite hopefully, "Through the Spirit we become intimate with God." Onlookers were struck by the unparalleled intimacy Jesus enjoyed with God, a closeness marked when he called God "Abba." The God who hurled the stars out into galaxies, who fashioned mountains and oceans, this same God was like a loving "daddy" to Jesus. But we are not stuck admiring their tenderness at a distance. No, "God, sent the Spirit of his Son into our hearts, crying 'Abba! Father!'" (Galatians 4:6). Notice we do not just take off on our own initiative and decide "I will be intimate with God." It is the Spirit who is sent into our souls by God, actually saying the words, weaving the relationship, stretching herself as a loving umbilical cord to God, so we gasp, swallow hard, and weep for joy, for we are (quite like Jesus) on intimate terms with God.

When Paul announced this same glorious news to the Romans, he wrote, "When we cry, 'Abba! Father!' it is the Spirit himself bearing witness with our spirit that we are children of God, and if children, then heirs, heirs of God ... provided we suffer with him in order that we may also be glorified with him" (Romans 8:16-17). The first two-thirds of this thought we sweetly cherish. By the Spirit we are "children of God," but not in some generalized humanitarian sense. Imagine the best, wisest, most affectionate, strong and passionately tender parent in history, holding his child in his lap, reading together, hugging; she strokes his hair and points out the window to an eagle soaring toward a distant mountain. Multiply this love by ninety-seven and you have a glimpse of what the Spirit is working overtime right now to give to you, to me, to all of us.

But that last phrase, "... provided we suffer with him." Woody Allen once joked, "I would prefer to achieve immortality without dying." Why did Jesus have to say "Take up your cross," and "Whoever would save his life will lose it" (Mark 8:34-35)? Like a hard elbow to the midsection that takes your breath, this paradox will not be yanked away from us by the Spirit. Intimacy with God requires that you burn bridges behind you, that you dare to walk into harm's way just as Jesus did, that you empty your cabinets and vaults and give Christ everything, for this alone is the way to have everything. Losing my life is the one and only narrow way for me to receive the one and only gift I ever really wanted. Do you remember what St. Augustine said? "The gift of the Holy Spirit is no more than the Holy Spirit."

The psalmist, in agony with nothing left to hang on to, prays to God in a way that probably elicits a smile from the Holy Spirit:

> Whom have I in heaven but thee?
>     And there is nothing upon earth that I desire
>         besides thee.
> My flesh and my heart may fail,
>     but God is the strength of my heart and my
>         portion for ever.
> For lo, those who are far from thee shall perish; . . .
> But for me it is good to be near God;
>     I have made the Lord GOD my refuge.
>                     (Psalm 73:25-28)

If we suffer with him, we will be glorified with him, and not just in the future. Thankfully there is comfort now.

# SENDING THE COMFORTER

*Come, Holy Spirit, promise of Jesus our Lord:*

*Stranded in the wilderness, I strain, then hear Your voice*

*that cries "Comfort!" You are my Comfort.*

*You anticipate the Comfort I need some time before*

*I am even aware of my need. I rest in You. Amen.*

The Gospel of John lingers over the after-dinner conversation Jesus shared with his disciples on the night before he gave himself up for us. Not merely sensing their anxious foreboding that night, but anticipating the terrible grief they would suffer the following day, and perhaps even preparing them for the brutal sorrows they would face over the next thirty years, Jesus loved them with words,

saying he would not leave them desolate, that he would send a Counselor, a Comforter, the Holy Spirit whose comfort is not just a sigh and a hug but the rock-solid truth of reality, the resurrection of Jesus, the hope that whatever sorrow we face will be turned into joy (John 14-16).

George Frideric Handel, reeling from depression, hounded by creditors, crushed by the failures of his operas, afflicted by rheumatism and then a stroke, was granted something like a miraculous vision. He put his finger on that startling prophecy to the despairing exiles and scribbled down the most lovely aria, as a tenor breaks the silence: "Comfort ye my people, saith your God; speak ye comfortably to Jerusalem, and cry unto her, that her warfare is accomplished, that her iniquity is pardoned" (Isaiah 40:1-2). In every wilderness, if we are still, if we listen, a voice cries "Comfort!" to us. For the Holy Spirit bears our anguish, our pain, our darkness. The Spirit feels the awful intensity of my anguish even before I notice it. And the Spirit gets busy right then, weaving a warm blanket of comfort to wrap us in God's unfailing love. St. Basil wrote that through the Spirit "hearts are lifted up, the infirm are held by the hand."

The Spirit's comfort is like no other. My spouse may listen and strive to grasp my inner turmoil, and she may hug and kiss me gently on the forehead. My friend may shed a tear and grope after some word to ease the pain. My pastor may read a psalm and set church folk to delivering casseroles. But the Spirit, who certainly relies heavily upon my spouse, my friend, and my pastor, the Spirit can go where no person can go, not even the wisest, most tender and sympathetic spouse or friend. The Spirit cuts into the marrow of my soul and understands my darkness even better than I do, feels it more profoundly than I do—and then the Spirit brings a comfort more powerful, more gentle, than any combination of hugs, words, or casseroles. The Spirit is God, the Spirit is love; and the Spirit comforts me not with any thing, but with the Spirit.

Martin Luther is not as soothing as we might like, but he tells the truth: "The name Comforter ... means that he must discharge his office at no place save where there is *no* comfort to be found and where comfort is needed and longed for. Therefore he cannot comfort hard heads and haughty hearts." Our hard heads may acknowledge our need for comfort at times, but perhaps the longest trek our hard heads cannot fathom making is the journey to joy.

# LESSON TWENTY-THREE

# THE SPIRIT AND JOY

*Come, Holy Spirit, my deepest unsatisfied Desire:*

*No gadget, no experience, no thing can deliver*

*that most elusive gift, Joy, which You alone bring.*

*To our sorrow and cynicism, You declare: "I beg to differ."*

*Help me to choose joy, and then relish the gift. Amen.*

People figure out how to have fun. The United States Constitution grants every American the right to "the pursuit of happiness." But no one needs to be told that all our endless rounds of fun, our diversions, our most zealous pursuits of happiness, no matter how successful, prove to be nothing more than a silly dance around a gaping hollow place in our souls. God made us for joy, which is deeper than happiness, or maybe different entirely from happiness and fun. Joy isn't happiness times two or a really tall pile of fun.

Joy is counter-cultural and is downright scandalous in a world hardened by cynicism. Joy is a defiant smile in the face of the worst bad luck, for joy is the Spirit's whispered secret that we are nestled quite securely in God's loving hand. Joy can weather unhappiness. In fact, joy is frequently discovered in the middle of sorrow. The widow smiles at the sight of her childhood friend's tears while they lift their voices at the funeral, singing

'Tis grace hath brought me safe thus far and grace will lead me home.

In one sense, we choose joy. We forever stumble upon some fork in the road, and we can choose joy or choose to be resentful. And yet the very choice of joy is a gift of the Spirit, who is forever beckoning, coaxing me toward joy. When joy pokes its surprising head into my life, I know I could not have won this myself. In fact, joy is barricaded from my heart by sin, by pride, by my sense of self-entitlement. That barricade must be torn down, by confession, by humility, by a profound sense of gratitude for even the smallest little gift I might have taken for granted five minutes earlier.

Some seasoning is required for the Spirit's gift of joy to become more a reality. Evelyn Underhill notes that "it is rather immature to be upset about the weather, yet very few souls tranquilly pursue the spiritual course without minding the spiritual weather. Here too we must expect fog, cold, persistent cloudiness, gales, and sudden stinging hail, as well as the sun." Joy is about consistency in the spiritual life. Since joy is different from the emotion of happiness, then we need not expect joy to evaporate when God seems absent. Oscar Romero, the heroic archbishop who suffered brutally for his faith, said:

God is not failing us when we don't feel his presence....

God exists, and he exists even more, the farther you feel from him....

When you feel the anguished desire for God to come near because you don't feel him present, then God is very close to your anguish....

Let us learn ... that God is always our Father and never forsakes us, and that we are closer to him than we think.

Joy is always elusive, at least while we're still down on this planet. We taste joy, but the very taste whets our appetite for more. C .S. Lewis defined joy as "an unsatisfied desire which is itself more desirable than any other satisfaction." We live in this in-between zone defined by 1 Peter 1:6-8: "In this you rejoice, though now for a little while you may have to suffer various trials, so that the genuineness of your faith, more precious than gold which though perishable is tested by fire, may redound to praise ... of Jesus Christ. Without having seen him you love him ... and you believe in him and rejoice with unutterable and exalted joy." For joy is finally all about hope. But before we get to hope, we must turn to the foundation of hope.

# THE SPIRIT OF TRUTH

*Come, Holy Spirit, the Truth which sets us free:*

*I will settle for nothing less than the Truth,*

*for You are the Truth, and Your Truth is beautiful.*

*Expose all lies, all pretending, every charade.*

*Whet my appetite for what is true and good, for You. Amen.*

A fter supper on the night before his crucifixion, Jesus was fixated on the issue of truth, and his parting pledge to his friends was that he would send the Holy Spirit, who will teach all things, telling the truth about God the Father, Jesus the Son, sin, judgment, and hope. "When the Spirit of truth comes, he will guide you into all the truth" (John 16:13). For readers in the twenty-first century, Jesus would underline that word *truth*, for we live in a world where truth does not matter half so much as effectiveness, productivity, getting ahead. In the realm of religion, truth now is a private, personal matter of mere opinion. But the Holy Spirit is redoubling her efforts to cry out that there is such a thing as truth, that truth matters, that truth comes through the Spirit, that the Spirit is truth. As St. Basil put it so eloquently, the Spirit is "the source of sanctification, spiritual light, who gives illumination to everyone using His powers to search for the truth—and the illumination He gives us is Himself."

Christians need never fear truth, no matter where it appears, in science, philosophy, or even poetry (didn't Keats say "Beauty is truth, truth beauty"?). The Spirit spreads truth around generously, not stingily. Jonathan Edwards even believed that Socrates, Plato, and the ancient Chinese philosophers were inspired by the Holy Spirit to say "such wonderful things." Clark Pinnock even believes the Spirit works in other religions: "It would be strange if the Spirit excused himself from the very arena of culture where people search for meaning. If God is reaching out to sinners, it is hard to comprehend why he would not do so in the sphere of religion.... Though Jesus is not named in other faiths, the Spirit is present and may be experienced." Not that other religions are therefore the full truth, but the Spirit simply cannot enjoy truth if truth is boxed away or doled out only parsimoniously.

We need to be taught. We do not possess the truth genetically, and we flail helplessly if we try titanically to be arbiters of what is true. Jesus said, "Blessed are the meek... Blessed are the pure in heart, for they shall see God" (Matthew 5:5, 8). Humility, a risky openness, never letting the steel trapdoor slam shut on our souls—these are the dispositions the Holy Spirit requires for us to be taught. Jesus added, "Blessed are those who hunger and thirst for righteousness" (Matthew 5:6), for we never possess the truth, but delight in the truth while forever hungering and thirsting for more.

The teaching function of the Spirit is twofold. Not only does the Spirit present truth to us, for instance in the words of Scripture, but also the same Spirit that inspired Scripture in the first place must open our ears and inspire us to hear and comprehend what is inspired. John Calvin declared that "the word will never gain credit in the hearts of men, till it be confirmed by the internal testimony of the Spirit."

We may recognize truth as hailing from the Holy Spirit when that truth is enveloped in love. The Spirit does not fire truth like bullets; the Spirit does not bludgeon us with truth of iron. Truth arrives lovingly, hopefully. Listen to St. Ephrem:

> Truth and love are wings that cannot be separated,
> for Truth without Love is unable to fly,
> so too Love without Truth is unable to soar up:
> their yoke is one of harmony.

The Spirit loves us with the truth, perhaps most helpfully when we must make decisions.

# THE SPIRIT AND DISCERNMENT

*Come, Holy Spirit, sharpen my discernment.*

*Instill in my heart a sense of Your direction;*

*purge every bogus rationale and selfish motive,*

*for my desire is to do Your will, at every turn*

*so my mind and life will be transformed by You. Amen.*

eloved, do not believe every spirit, but test the spirits to see whether they are of God" (1 John 4:1). We come to a major juncture in life and must decide, "Do I move to Des Moines?" "Do I marry Kevin?" "Should I change careers?" "Do we try the chemotherapy?"—and we pray for the Spirit to guide us. The Spirit, so loving, so eager for our good, leaps at the opportunity and mercifully kneads and shapes our thinking.

But not just on the big decisions! We have a thousand little turning points every day when we decide to go here or there, to buy this or save our money, to watch TV or go to Bible study, to bring up a difficult subject in conversation or just avoid it, to walk out and wave to the garbage collector or to hurry on to work. Discernment is not just about doing, but how we view the world. Do I fawn over all that is sleek and glittery, or do I admire earthy wisdom in low places? Do I react to a challenging situation with resentment or gratitude? Do I dream of a luxurious life or hunger for more humility? Do I thank God for the smallest gift or demand much? Do I stare at the curve of her body, or do I turn away?

When we test the spirits, we recall that every desire, every possibility is not of God. So we do not stupidly ask God to bless whatever we already want to do. We listen, and we expect that the Spirit will nudge us toward a thought or a behavior that frankly is odd in the eyes of the world, for the world is not of God. If we fit in too cozily in this world, then we are not discerning the Spirit. "Do not be conformed to this world but be transformed by the renewal of your mind, that you may prove what is the will of God, what is good and acceptable and perfect" (Romans 12:2).

You may pick up some bad advice about discernment, even from well-intending friends. One fallacy is that of the "open door." Someone says "The door was open, the job was available, so that means it was God's will." But there are countless open doors through which we should not walk. And God may call us to bang down some other door—which leads to a second fallacy.

Someone says, "Everything fell into place, and it was just so happy and pleasing to everyone, so it surely was God's will." But in the garden of Gethsemane, Jesus discerned the Spirit, and he was gruesomely nailed to a shaft of olive wood. Look at Jeremiah, John the Baptist, all the martyrs of the Church, saints and heroes through history who have tuned their souls to the Spirit, who have said yes to the Spirit and have suffered severly. Deep down, we do not really want to use the Spirit to make our lives comfortable. We want the Spirit to use us, for the Spirit to blow where it wills, for the Spirit to cast us into the fray where God needs us the most, for the Spirit to help us find those barbed points of conflict with an unsaved world.

Discernment comes through prayer, prayer, and more prayer. The Holy Spirit is like those wise trees in *The Lord of the Rings*, who speak Entish, "a lovely language, but it takes a very long time to say anything in it, because we do not say anything in it, unless it is worth taking a long time to say, and to listen to." The Spirit takes time to say what is worthwhile, so discernment involves patience.

We test whatever we think is the Spirit's leading against the Scriptures, for the Spirit will not lure us toward anything contrary to the Spirit's own written testimony. We talk openly with Christian friends, the kinds of friends who know God, who love us too much to flatter us, who dare to ask hard questions and prick us with challenging words. We will not have anything resembling a perfect record when it comes to discerning the spirits, and so we lean heavily, always, on forgiveness and on the tantalizing hope that God will use even our missteps for good. For the good the Spirit brings out of life is not immediate, but is only out there in the time we cannot yet see.

# THE SPIRIT AND THE FUTURE

*Come, Holy Spirit, Pledge of certain hope:*

*Wherever I am headed, You have already arrived*

*and are waiting for me there with open arms.*

*Prepare me for that "eternal weight of glory,"*

*so I may truly walk by faith, not by sight. Amen.*

Every time we strive for discernment, every time we believe, every time we take a step out of the house, our life in the Spirit is set in the context of a future that has not yet dawned, a future promised but not yet attained. What could be more encouraging than the words the Spirit whispered over Paul's shoulder in prison? "We are afflicted in every way, but not crushed, perplexed but not driven to despair, ... knowing that he who raised the Lord Jesus will raise us also.... So we do not lose heart.... For this slight momentary affliction is preparing for us an eternal weight of glory beyond all comparison, because we look not to the things that are seen but to the things that are unseen.... Here indeed we groan, ... we sigh, ... so that what is mortal may be swallowed up by life. He who has prepared us for this very thing is God, who has given us the Spirit as a guarantee. So we are always of good courage, ... for we walk by faith, not by sight" (2 Corinthians 4:5–5:7).

Mind you, this future orientation is counter-intuitive, especially in American culture where we measure everything by results. We want possession now; we walk by sight. "Show me the money!" So in worldly measures, the Spirit will disappoint you every time. But if we could climb inside some huge lens and zoom out, way out so we could glimpse all of time and all of space, we would put our money not on what I get this afternoon but on what God has for me three decades or seventeen millennia out.

For the Spirit has little patience with vapid "optimism," the naïve view that "things will be better tomorrow." Things may well be worse tomorrow. The Spirit is hope, and hope is never naïve, but is always braced to weather whatever storm may come. Without the Spirit we have good reason to grab all we can get now, and every good reason to be wary, fearful, even terrified by the future. The Holy Spirit firmly invades all our grasping and fright, calmly lifting our gaze to God's marvelous future, a guarantee that we already enjoy a secure place in God's future, a future that can be calculated at something like the best day we could concoct in our wildest imagination—times a hundred and ninety-four (to the seventh power). St. Basil understood the climax of the Spirit's mission: "Through the Holy Spirit comes our restoration to Paradise, our ascension to the Kingdom of heaven, our adoption as God's sons, ... sharing in eternal glory." We are made for glory—I am, you are, and she is too. So everything looks so very different, but only through the eyes of faith, the Spirit's glimmer.

No disaster, however cataclysmic or abysmal, can undo the Spirit's ultimate plan. In olden times, the prophet Ezekiel was caught up in the Spirit and saw a grotesque valley strewn with dead bones. But the mighty Spirit rushed and swirled through the valley; and the bones rattled, moved, joined, sinews forming, flesh clothing, until life stood up, dancing, leaping for joy. So we can calm down. We can smile in the claws of sorrow, for Paul's yearning is answered: "May the God of hope fill you with all joy and peace in believing, so that by the power of the Holy Spirit you may abound in hope" (Romans 15:13).

# THE SPIRIT AND FREEDOM

*Come, Holy Spirit; You are our freedom.*

*Without You we are trapped in awful bondage*

*to sin, self, hollowness, hopelessness, loneliness.*

*Set us free, free to know, trust, and follow You,*

*so we may love You truly and joyfully forever. Amen.*

So at the end of the day, life in the Spirit is given over to awe, wonder, waiting, hope, yearning, prayer, yielding. Lesslie Newbigin, who witnessed the Spirit's dynamic work all over the world, wrote, "That surrender, that 'Amen,' is faith. And it is the work of the Holy Spirit. ... From God's side, it is the work of the Spirit; from my side it is faith.... Only God Himself has the power to bring my stubborn and rebellious will to the point of surrender." Perhaps the best way to conclude this exploration of the Holy Spirit is to speak of freedom. Karl Barth said that "to live in the Spirit means being set free and being permitted to live in freedom." What a rude slap in the face, the Spirit's bizarre suggestion that I am not free. Of course I am free! That's the greatness of humanity, isn't it? Soldiers defend freedom, and we celebrate freedom; we boast of freedom.

But the Spirit places a loving arm around our shoulder and urges us not to brag. If I am free in some way, the Spirit exposes the awful truth that I have squandered my freedom. I am free to mess up, free to get shackled to habits that are not of God, and I exercise that freedom with abandon. My so-called freedom reminds me of Prometheus, who scaled the heights and stole fire from the gods. Hurrah! I've made it to the top! But what was Prometheus's fate? Chained to the rocky Caucasus, vultures swarming in every night to gnaw on his guts. I am free only like the prisoner is free, choosing to wander about the cell, yet forever behind bars.

The Spirit sets us free: free from sin, free from hollowness, free from pointlessness, free from our proclivity to wound each other, free from sorrow. The Spirit sets us free: free for love, free to trust, free to serve, free to experience the beauty of life with God, a life I get a little glimpse of now, a life I welcome as promise, a life I will enjoy fully forever. Free to discover a profoundly personal relationship with Freedom itself, the Spirit, who freely brooded over the waters and fashioned a world, who freely spoke through the prophets, who freely descended dovelike on the son Jesus, who freely rushed on Jesus' disciples at Pentecost and still rushes on us, who freely makes love a reality, *the* reality. The Spirit sets us free to pray, for prayer in the Spirit is life. So we join with Christians through the centuries who in worship and solitude have uttered confidently these words from Rhabanus Maurus:

Come, pour thy joys on human kind;
From sin and sorrow set us free,
And make thy temples worthy thee.
Make us eternal truths receive,
And practise all that we believe.

# WORKS CITED

## Lesson 2: The Spirit Is Love

John Burnaby, trans., *Augustine: Later Works* (Philadelphia: The Westminster Press, 1955), p. 165. (author's rendition)

Kilian Walsh, trans., *The Works of Bernard of Clairvaux*, vol. 2, *Song of Songs I* (Kalamazoo, Mich.: Cistercian Publications, 1979), p. 46.

## Lesson 3: The Spirit in the Trinity

Ann Patchett, *bel canto: a novel* (New York: HarperCollins, 2001), p. 207.

Clark H. Pinnock, *Flame of Love: A Theology of the Holy Spirit* (Downers Grove, Ill.: InterVarsity Press, 1996), p. 31.

## Lesson 4: The Beauty of Anonymity

Robert W. Jenson, *America's Theologian: A Recommedation of Jonathan Edwards* (New York: Oxford University Press, 1988), p. 95.

Clark H. Pinnock, *Flame of Love: A Theology of the Holy Spirit* (Downers Grove, Ill.: InterVarsity Press, 1996), pp. 39-40.

## Lesson 5: The Inspiration of Scripture

Heinrich Bornkamm, *Luther and the Old Testament*, trans. Eric W. and Ruth C. Gritsch, ed. Victor I. Gruhn (Philadelphia: Fortress Press, 1969), pp. 86-87.

## Lesson 6: Jesus and the Holy Spirit

Heinrich Bornkamm, *Luther and the Old Testament*, trans. Eric W. and Ruth C. Gritsch, ed. Victor I. Gruhn (Philadelphia: Fortress Press, 1969), p. 86.

Clark H. Pinnock, *Flame of Love: A Theology of the Holy Spirit* (Downers Grove, Ill.: InterVarsity Press, 1996), p. 85.

## Lesson 7: Prayer and the Spirit

Frederick Buechner, *Wishful Thinking: A Theological ABC* (New York: Harper & Row, 1973), pp. 85-86.

Richard Robert Osmer, *A Teachable Spirit: Recovering the Teaching Office in the Church* (Louisville: Westminster/John Knox , 1990), p. 52.

Evelyn Underhill, *The Ways of the Spirit,* ed. Grace Adolphsen Brame (New York: Crossroad, 1996), p. 106.

## Lesson 8: The Spirit and Creation

Annie Dillard, *Pilgrim at Tinker Creek* (New York: Harper & Row, 1990), p. 135.

John Polkinghorne, *Serious Talk: Science and Religion in Dialogue* (Valley Forge, Penn.: Trinity, 1995), p. 45.

## Lesson 10: The Spirit and Feeling

Evelyn Underhill, *The Ways of the Spirit,* ed. Grace Adolphsen Brame (New York: Crossroad, 1996), p. 62.

## Lesson 11: The Conviction of Sin

Andrew Reed, written 1817.

Evelyn Underhill, *The Ways of the Spirit,* ed. Grace Adolphsen Brame (New York: Crossroad, 1996), p. 160.

## Lesson 12: The Spirit and Sanctification

Anonymous, "Away in a Manger," from Luke 2:7.

Gordon D. Fee, *God's Empowering Presence: The Holy Spirit in the Letters of Paul* (Peabody, Mass.: Hendrickson, 1994), p. 878.

Basil the Great, *On the Holy Spirit* (Crestwood, N.Y.: St. Vladimir's Seminary Press, 2001), 63.

## Lesson 13: Culture and the Spirit

Philip D. Kenneson, *Life on the Vine* (Downers Grove, Ill.: InterVarsity, 1999), p. 37.

## Lesson 14: The Spirit as Creator

Hildegard of Bingen, *Mystical Writings,* ed. Fiona Bowie and Oliver Davies (New York: Crossroad, 1990), p. 118.

Clark H. Pinnock, *Flame of Love: A Theology of the Holy Spirit* (Downers Grove, Ill.: InterVarsity Press, 1996), p. 50.

## Lesson 15: History and the Spirit

Karl Heim, *The Transformation of the Scientific World View* (New York: Harper & Bros., 1953), p. 21.

Reinhold Niebuhr, *The Irony of American History* (New York: Charles Scribner's Sons, 1952), p. 63.

## Lesson 16: The Spirit in the Church

Frederick Buechner, *The Clown in the Belfry: Writings on Faith and Fiction* (San Francisco: HarperSanFrancisco, 1992), p. 158.

## Lesson 17: Worship in the Spirit

Annie Dillard, *Holy the Firm* (New York: Harper & Row, 1977), p. 58.

James Weldon Johnson, *God's Trombones: Seven Negro Sermons in Verse* (New York: Penguin Books, 1972).

Sebastian Brock, *The Luminous Eye: The Spiritual World Vision of Saint Ephrem* (Kalamazoo, Mich.: Cistercian Publications, 1985), p. 104.

## Lesson 18: The Experience of Pentecostalism

Frank Bartleman, "Power in a Pentecostal Congregation," in *The Company of Preachers*, ed. Richard Lischer (Grand Rapids, Mich.: William B. Eerdmans, 2002), p. 418.

## Lesson 19: Unity in the Spirit

Cyril of Alexandria, Saint, (d. 444).

## Lesson 20: Discovering Your Calling

Jürgen Moltmann, *The Source of Life: The Holy Spirit and the Theology of Life* (Minneapolis: Fortress, 1997), p. 59.

Ernest Hemingway, *A Farewell to Arms*.

## Lesson 21: Intimacy with God

Basil the Great, *On the Holy Spirit* (Crestwood, N.Y.: St. Vladimir's Seminary Press, 2001), 77.

John Burnaby, trans., *Augustine: Later Works* (Philadelphia: The Westminster Press, 1955), p. 165. (author's rendition)

## Lesson 22: Sending the Comforter

George Friedrich Handel, "Comfort Ye My People."
Basil the Great, *On the Holy Spirit* (Crestwood, N.Y.: St. Vladimir's Seminary Press, 2001), 44.
Heinrich Bornkamm, *Luther and the Old Testament*, trans. Eric W. and Ruth C. Gritsch, ed. Victor I. Gruhn (Philadelphia: Fortress Press, 1969), p. 27.

## Lesson 23: The Spirit and Joy

John Newton, "Amazing Grace," 1779.
Evelyn Underhill, *The Ways of the Spirit*, ed. Grace Adolphsen Brame (New York: Crossroad, 1996), p. 173.
Oscar Romero, *The Violence of Love*, trans. James R. Brockman, S. J. (Farmington, Penn.: Plough Publishing, 1988), p. 131.
C. S. Lewis, *Surprised by Joy* (San Diego: Harcourt Brace & Co., 1966).

## Lesson 24: The Spirit of Truth

Basil the Great, *On the Holy Spirit* (Crestwood, N.Y.: St. Vladimir's Seminary Press, 2001), 43.
Robert W. Jenson, *America's Theologian: A Recommendation of Jonathan Edwards* (New: Oxford University Press, 1988), p. 129.
Clark H. Pinnock, *Flame of Love: A Theology of the Holy Spirit* (Downers Grove, Ill.: InterVarsity Press, 1996), p. 203.
Hugh T. Kerr, ed., *A Compend of the Institutes of the Christian Religion by John Calvin* (Philadelphia: The Westminster Press, 1964), p. 16.
Sebastian Brock, *The Luminous Eye: The Spiritual World Vision of Saint Ephreme* (Kalamazoo, Mich.: Cistercian Publications, 1985), p. 104.

## Lesson 26: The Spirit and the Future

Basil the Great, *On the Holy Spirit* (Crestwood, N.Y.: St. Vladimir's Seminary Press, 2001), 59.

## Lesson 27: The Spirit and Freedom

Geoffrey Wainwright, *Lesslie Newbigin: A Theological Life* (Oxford: Oxford University Press, 2000), pp. 46-47.
Karl Barth, *Dogmatics in Outline* (New York: Harper & Row, 1959), p. 138.

# INDEX OF AUTHORS QUOTED

# A GUIDE FOR SMALL GROUPS

*Kenneth H. Carter, Jr.*

J ames Howell offers the reader twenty-seven meditations on an elusive subject, the Holy Spirit. When you have spent time in these pages you will not have mastered the subject, and that is precisely the point ("*The Holy Spirit is not anything you 'have,' for the Holy Spirit is too big, too marvelous, too treacherous, to be boxed inside me or even the most spiritual person on the planet*"—lesson 1). It will help, at the beginning, to lay aside our stereotypes about the Holy Spirit and the cultural expectations surrounding immediate results, dramatic feelings, and individual experience. The author is guiding us toward an appreciation of the Holy Spirit that is rooted in a deep reading of Scripture and tradition. Allow the author, and those who are cited, and the Holy Spirit to speak to you as you read and reflect.

It will also be helpful to meditate on this material in the context of a small group. In the New Testament it is clear

that the Holy Spirit is at work in the Body of Christ
(1 Corinthians 12–14), and the author makes a strong case
for the fundamental relationship between church and Holy
Spirit (see lesson 16, "The Spirit in the Church"). Of course,
the small group could take the form of a Sunday school
class, a worship committee, an Emmaus Reunion group, a
Covenant Discipleship group, a women's circle, or an early
morning Bible study. Any group that is grounded in the
Christian experience would benefit from Howell's reflections on the Holy Spirit, a subject that is at once essential
and yet also misunderstood. A word might be appropriate,
however, about the unique challenges of leading a group on
the subject of the Holy Spirit!

# LEADING A SMALL GROUP

A small group focusing on *The Kiss of God: 27 Lessons on
the Holy Spirit* will need a leader or convener. Of course the
Holy Spirit is the leader, but the Spirit also uses our gifts in
the functioning of our life together. As a convener, you will
have the following responsibilities:

- Invite participants into the group experience.
- Interpret the study as an attempt to gain a
  greater appreciation of an essential but also misunderstood, and perhaps neglected subject.
- Establish a group climate of support and
  accountability. Reassure participants that their
  experiences will be honored in the group, but
  also challenge them to consider perspectives that
  might be new or different to them.

The following guidelines might also help in the calling
together of the group.

- Seek out individuals who are united by a common interest in the faith, but different in their expressions of it (a reading of lesson 19, "Unity of the Spirit," might be good background for this task). Think of individuals who do not naturally pray together, study together, serve together, or even worship together. A diversity of participants will enrich the experience of the Spirit in the group meetings.
- Establish an atmosphere of trust and acceptance. As Howell writes in lesson 21, the Holy Spirit is about "Intimacy with God." And so the development of a secure and even confidential community will enhance the willingness of participants to share their gifts, to bear one another's burdens, and to acknowledge the movement of the Spirit in their lives.

You might want to draft a simple covenant that will guide the group's experience in the coming sessions. The covenant might touch on the following matters:

- A willingness to listen attentively to others.
- A commitment to keep the discussion that is shared in the group confidential.
- A decision to make attendance at the gatherings a priority in the participant's time schedule.
- A determination to lay aside stereotypes and preconceptions about the meaning of the Holy Spirit.
- A receptivity to an outpouring of the Spirit and a resolution to cultivate the fruit of the Spirit (Galatians 5) that might grow as the study unfolds.

# THE ORGANIZATION OF THE LESSONS

The following format will allow the group to meet together in four sessions. These might be once a week for four weeks. The advantage of this pattern is that individuals have time to reflect on the material over a period of several days. You might also consider adapting *The Kiss of God* to a retreat format, with the four meetings taking place on Friday evening, Saturday morning, Saturday afternoon, and Saturday evening. Whichever format is chosen, it is important not to race through the material. Instead, allow James Howell and the voices of Scripture and tradition to speak, and give ample time for the fruit of the Spirit (Galatians 5) to ripen.

# SESSION ONE (Lessons 1-7)

## *Defining the Holy Spirit*

Begin by allowing the participants to introduce themselves. Ask them to open their copy of *The Kiss of God* to the first lesson, and point them to the prayer, which begins with the refrain "Come, Holy Spirit." This refrain invites the participant to assume a posture of receptivity and openness to new life and new birth. The convener might then invite the group to join together in a common reading of the opening prayer at the beginning of the first lesson ("Who Is the Holy Spirit?").

You might begin with the following questions:

- When you hear the words *Holy Spirit*, what images form in your mind?
- How would you complete this sentence: The Holy Spirit is present when _____.

The Hebrew word for *spirit* can also be translated as "wind" or "breath." What connotations or meanings are associated with these words among the participants? Some examples might be the feeling of shortness of breath, the invisibility of wind but the visibility of its effects, the chaos of wind, and so forth. The author also notes that the Hebrew word for spirit, *ruach,* is feminine. Is this a new understanding for participants? How might this understanding enrich our perception of God?

A strong emphasis in the first lesson is the inability of an individual, no matter how mature, to control or possess the Spirit? Do you agree? Disagree? Why?

## The Holy Spirit and Love

Ask a member ahead of time to read 1 Corinthians 13, or invite the group to sing "The Gift of Love." (You will need to have copies of the hymn available.) Then ask members of the group, in silence, to read the opening prayer in lesson 2 ("The Spirit Is Love"). Ask them to circle any word or phrase that seems especially significant or surprising to them.

After summarizing the relationship between love and the spirit, ask participants to share what they perceived to be important in the opening prayer.

## The Spirit and the Trinity

While most discussions of the Trinity are on a fairly high intellectual plane, all Christians can (and should) reflect on the relationship between the Father, the Son, and the Holy Spirit.

- Ask participants to silently read John 14–17 and offer any insights or comments that come to them.

Howell employs the image of the *perichoresis* from the writings of early Christian theologians, likening it to a dance (lesson 3). Was this image helpful to you? Why or why not?

In the relation of Father, Son, and Holy Spirit, the latter term is described as beautiful, humble, and even anonymous. Can you recall an experience of the Spirit (such as the one Howell mentions in lesson 4)?

## Scripture, Jesus, and Prayer

In this segment of the first gathering several critical issues are raised: the inspiration of Scripture, the relation of Jesus to the Spirit, the role of the Spirit in prayer. After noting the meaning of inspired as "breathed in," invite a participant to read 2 Timothy 3:16 (quoted in lesson 5, "The Inspiration of Scripture"). Then ask if any can recall experiences with reading the Bible in which they felt corrected, educated, or equipped for some purpose, perhaps by reading the Bible devotionally or hearing a teacher or preacher offer a new insight?

In Luke 4, Jesus is "led by the Spirit" into the wilderness. Later, speaking in Nazareth, he announces that "the spirit of the Lord is upon me." How do you see the Spirit at work in the life of Jesus? How do you see the Spirit at work in individuals who follow Jesus today?

We do not know how to pray, Paul writes, but "the Spirit helps us in our weakness" (Romans 8:26). In light of your reading and conversation thus far, how might the Spirit help you to pray?

Conclude the first session by saying together the prayer at the beginning of lesson 7 ("Prayer and the Spirit").

# Session Two (Lessons 8-14)

The Spirit is at work in our lives, sometimes in quiet and compelling ways. Thank participants for their commitment to the group and to the exploration of person and work of the Holy Spirit in their lives.

Begin with a reading of Genesis 1:1–2:3. Then invite the group to say together the words of the opening prayer (lesson 8, "The Spirit and Creation").

In lesson 8, the author offers the following wisdom: "To know the Spirit we look to creation, big and small." Invite participants, in groups of two or three, to reflect on spiritual experiences that were occasioned by the creation of God (examples might be the birth of a child, the sound of a friend's laughter, hiking across a mountain, or walking along a beach, and so forth).

The creation helps us to understand that "God is patient and subtle" (lesson 8). Recall an experience when you were engaged in a creative act. How was the virtue of patience present or absent?

The Spirit is not so much in us, the author insists, as "we are in the Spirit." And yet he acknowledges that "the Spirit works from the inside out" (lesson 9). Can you recall an inner experience of the Spirit in your journey? Howell then meditates on the limitations of trusting our feelings as the work of the Spirit. How might our feelings be an unreliable indicator of the movement of God in our lives?

Lesson 11 focuses on "The Conviction of Sin." Bring to the group a copy of your denomination's creeds or statements of faith, including prayers of confession. Ask the following questions:

- Why is confession of sin important?
- Why is corporate confession of sin important?
- What do we lose in worship if confession is omitted?

Ask the participants to read aloud the opening prayer in this lesson together. Taking a few moments of silence, ask them once again to circle or underline any word or phrase that has particular relevance or meaning for them.

Lessons 12 and 13 connect the call to holiness with our challenge to live in the world "but not of it." Ask for any comments or insights gained from the reading of these two meditations.

Lesson 14 returns to the theme of creation, and the task of praising God. Ask one of the participants to read Psalm 104:1-13. Conclude with a group reading of the prayer at the beginning of lesson 14.

# SESSION THREE (Lessons 15-20)

Begin with a common reading of the prayer from lesson 15 ("History and the Spirit"). Ask individuals, at this midpoint of the study, to list any new learnings about the Holy Spirit.

Then move to a discussion of the role of the Spirit in the events of history. Reflect on current events or recent historical movements that seem to be the work of the Spirit (the end of apartheid in South Africa, for example). Howell insists that "history is not random." How might God be at work at this time in our history?

## The Church and Worship

Take a moment to read lesson 16 ("The Spirit in the Church") in silence. In groups of two or three, recall ways in which the Spirit has been at work in your congregation. Following the author's insights, you may remember incidents that have been surprising in ways and mundane in others. In the last paragraph of lesson 16, Howell makes a statement that is worthy of discussion: "When we praise God in eternity, I will not sing solo, and neither shall you."

Ask participants to reflect on the social character of the Holy Spirit.

This leads into the role of the Holy Spirit in worship (lesson 17). Invite participants to discuss experiences of the spirit in the hearing of the Word and the sharing of the sacraments (Baptism and Communion). Howell's discussion of Pentecostalism (lesson 18) provides a balanced perspective on an often misunderstood topic. Allow time for discussion of this lesson.

## *The Spirit and the Body: Unity and Call*

We are a part of the universal Church, and yet we express our faith within a particular tradition. We are called to follow Christ and his teachings, and yet we have gifts that differ and allow us to serve in a variety of ways. There is a rich diversity of traditions, denominations, and churches within the Christian faith. There are an infinite number of ways that we might respond to the call of God. The differences in our churches may seem to be a sign of human political failure. The brokenness in our lives may seem to be an experience of God's abandonment. And yet, Howell insists, the Spirit is at work even here. Ask participants to reflect silently on the work of God, even amidst human division and brokenness. Conclude with a common reading of the prayer in lesson 19 ("Unity in the Spirit") and a singing of the chorus, "They Will Know We Are Christians by Our Love."

# SESSION FOUR (Lessons 21-27)

Begin with two scripture readings: Romans 8:14-17 and John 14:18-19, 25-27. Ask participants to pray, in silence, the simple words: "Come, Holy Spirit."

## The Intimacy of the Comforter

The final gathering begins with attention to the role of the Spirit in the life of the person who struggles. Jesus promises to send the Holy Spirit, the comforter, to us. The author describes this comforter as One who works through friends, family, pastors, and church members, but also in ways that are beyond our human efforts.

In groups of two or three, reflect on the following questions:

- How has the Holy Spirit been a source of comfort in your own life?
- How is dependence upon the Holy Spirit easy? Or difficult?

## Joy, Truth, and Discernment

The author comments on the distinction between joy and happiness (lesson 23). Give participants an opportunity to respond to this important concept.

The Spirit will guide us into the truth, Jesus promised (John 16:13). The Spirit was at work in guiding the formation of Scripture, and the Spirit is at work in helping us to understand Scripture. Ask participants to recall an experience when the teaching or reading of Scripture seemed inspired.

Take a few moments to lead participants through lesson 25 ("The Spirit and Discernment"). What does it mean to "test the spirits"? How can Jesus be our guide in the discernment of spirits?

## Future and Freedom

Howell reflects in lesson 26 on the difference between hope and optimism. He mentions Ezekiel and the apostle Paul as examples of individuals who were hopeful in the midst of almost hopeless circumstances. How can the distinction between hope and optimism help you in facing difficult situations?

Finally, ask individuals to read the paragraph beginning with the words "The Spirit sets us free" in lesson 27 ("The Spirit and Freedom"). How has this freedom become a reality in our lives? How might we enter more fully into this freedom? What might we need to relinquish in order to experience this kind of freedom?

Conclude with a prayer of thanksgiving for God's gift of the Holy Spirit, and share the peace of Christ as you depart.